Your Guide to Government

What is a Government?

Baron Bedesky

Crabtree Publishing Company

www.crabtreebooks.com

Crabtree Publishing Company

www.crabtreebooks.com

Author: Baron Bedesky
Coordinating editor: Chester Fisher
Series editor: Scholastic Ventures
Project manager: Kavita Lad (Q2AMEDIA)
Art direction: Dibakar Acharjee (Q2AMEDIA)
Cover design: Nikhil Bhutani (Q2AMEDIA)
Design: Ruchi Sharma (Q2AMEDIA)
Photo research: Sejal Sehgal Wani (Q2AMEDIA)
Editor: Molly Aloian
Proofreader: Crystal Sikkens
Project coordinator: Robert Walker
Production coordinator: Katherine Berti
Font management: Mike Golka
Prepress technician: Ken Wright

Photographs:

Cover: Ron Edmonds/Associated Press, J. Helgason/Shutterstock (background); Title page: JustASC/Shutterstock; P4: Associated Press; P5: Jose Gil/Shutterstock; P6: Maciej Oleksy/Shutterstock; P7: Associated Press; P8: Associated Press; P9: Tom Antos/Shutterstock; P10: Associated Press; P11: DoD Media; P12(l): Tomasz Szymanski/ Shutterstock; P12(c): Condor 36/Shutterstock; P12(r): Dolby1985/Dreamstime; P13: Dennis MacDonald/Alamy; P14: Duncan Walker/Istockphoto; P15: ScPhotog/Bigstockphoto; P16: Loc Prints and Photographic Division; P17(t): Associated Press; P17(c): Associated Press; P18: Ian Dagnall/Alamy; P19: ACshots/Bigstockphoto; P20: James Steidl/Shutterstock; P21: Jonathan Larsen/Shutterstock; P22: Jaimie Duplass/Shutterstock; P23: Associated Press; P24: Cheryl Casey/Shutterstock; P25: Naomi Bassitt/Istockphoto; P26: Eric1513/Dreamstime; P27: 1amg/Bigstockphoto; P28: Associated Press; P29: Arpad Benedek/Istockphoto; P30: Pavel Losevsky/Istockphoto; P31: Iphoto/Fotolia

Illustrations:
P12: Q2A Media Art Bank

Library and Archives Canada Cataloguing in Publication

Bedesky, Baron
    What is a government? / Baron Bedesky.

(Your guide to government)
Includes index.
ISBN 978-0-7787-4328-6 (bound).--ISBN 978-0-7787-4333-0 (pbk.)

    1. United States--Politics and government--Juvenile literature.
I. Title. II. Series.

JK40.B435 2008   j320.473   C2008-904468-1

Library of Congress Cataloging-in-Publication Data

Bedesky, Baron.
    What is a government? / Baron Bedesky.
        p. cm. -- (Your guide to government)
    Includes index.
    ISBN-13: 978-0-7787-4333-0 (pbk. : alk. paper)
    ISBN-10: 0-7787-4333-0 (pbk. : alk. paper)
    ISBN-13: 978-0-7787-4328-6 (reinforced library binding : alk. paper)
    ISBN-10: 0-7787-4328-4 (reinforced library binding : alk. paper)
    1. Public administration--Juvenile literature. I. Title.

JF1351.B43 2009
320.4--dc22
                                    2008030909

Crabtree Publishing Company

www.crabtreebooks.com   1-800-387-7650

Printed in Canada/012021/MA20210113

Published in Canada
Crabtree Publishing
616 Welland Ave.
St. Catharines, ON
L2M 5V6

Published in the United States
Crabtree Publishing
PMB 59051
350 Fifth Avenue, 59th Floor
New York, New York 10118

Published in the United Kingdom
Crabtree Publishing
Maritime House
Basin Road North, Hove
BN41 1WR

Published in Australia
Crabtree Publishing
3 Charles Street
Coburg North
VIC, 3058

Contents

Governments

A **government** is people who help us every day. These people work very hard as part of a team. You see the government at work in your own **community,** or the area where you live. We need many government teams in our community and country. These teams work together.

A government runs a school, a city, a state, or a country. It makes decisions because it is in charge. A government keeps us safe and decides what we need most in our lives. People in government also listen to us. We share ideas and work on important jobs.

A government makes decisions for the people it oversees.

Governments keep citizens safe. The police work for the government.

The president of the United States leads our country. The governor leads your state. Your community has government leaders, too. The **mayor** leads the city. The police chief, the sheriff, and the fire chief are other leaders who make your neighborhood a better place.

We Need Them

We need a government to make **laws**. Laws are rules that keep us safe and help us work together. A government also makes sure we all follow those laws. Even easy things cannot be done without laws. For example, would you want to cross the street if people drove their cars too fast?

A government tells us what is important in our community. We listen to what they suggest. If people agree with the idea, these leaders get the job done. A mayor might say the town needs a new fire truck. If people agree, the town can buy the truck.

These people are voting. People make their opinions known by voting. Governments must listen to what voters say.

Every government represents many people. Government leaders need to know what is best for all those people.

A government helps run your school. They hire the people that watch over all of the schools in a **district**. They make decisions about what books to use. The government pays for the teachers and buildings, as well.

Our Neighborhood

Our government wants us all to be safe. It builds police stations and fire stations. It also builds our hospitals and clinics. The government helps after a disaster. It helps take care of the old and sick.

The government has a plan for what you will learn at school. Children in the same grade should learn the same things at the same time. Your teachers use this plan in your class. The plan also says you should get exercise and spend time outside every day.

The government will help people during a disaster. During this flood, the government sent rescuers to people in danger.

The government built the roads we drive on every day.

The government builds our roads, streets, and sidewalks. It puts up street signs and stop lights. If you ride a city bus or a subway, you can thank the government. It also runs our parks and makes sure we have clean water to drink.

FACT BOX

Basketball star Shaquille O'Neal works for the government. He works with the police in Miami, Florida and Tempe, Arizona.

9

Our Country

Our country must protect its people. Our government has an army, a navy, and an air force to do this. Together, these groups form the **military**. The men and women in the military protect us. They also help other countries and protect people who live there.

If a person cannot not find a job, he or she may get some money from the government. This will help the person until he or she finds work.

Some communities need more homes. The government may help build them. People who do not have places to stay can live there.

The judge sits in front of a court and listens to both sides speak.

The military protects the land, skies, and seas. This aircraft carrier protects many people.

Our government has many laws. If anyone breaks the law, they may go to court. The person in charge of a court is called a **judge**. The judge listens to what everyone has to say. Then the judge decides who is right or wrong. The person who is wrong may be punished for what he or she has done.

Three Branches

In the United States, the government has three different **branches,** or parts. We call them the **legislative** branch, the **executive** branch, and the **judicial** branch.

The legislative branch makes all the laws. The executive branch makes sure people obey the laws. The courts make up the judicial branch. A court decides if a law has been followed correctly.

Every government has all three branches. The mayor leads the executive branch of the city government. Many people also work in the legislative branch.

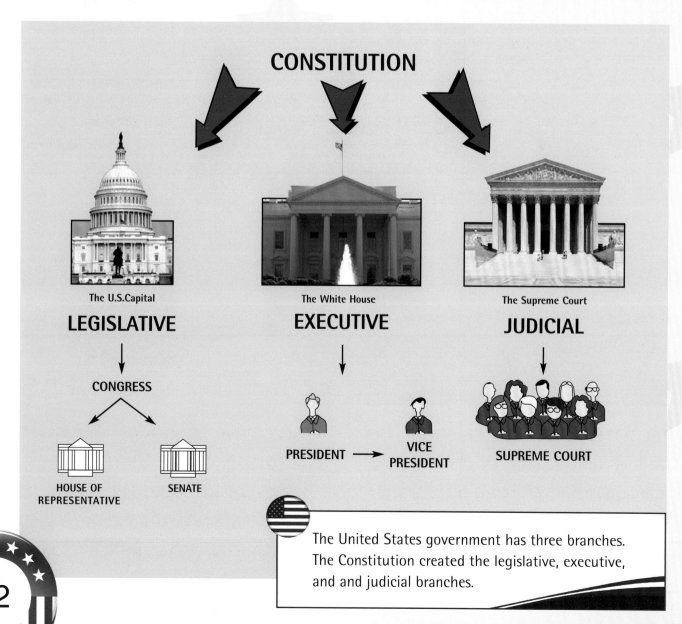

CONSTITUTION

The U.S.Capital
LEGISLATIVE

CONGRESS

HOUSE OF
REPRESENTATIVE

SENATE

The White House
EXECUTIVE

PRESIDENT → VICE
PRESIDENT

The Supreme Court
JUDICIAL

SUPREME COURT

The United States government has three branches. The Constitution created the legislative, executive, and and judicial branches.

This meter reader works for the executive branch. She is enforcing a law.

The legislative branch suggests new laws for the city or town. The city's judicial branch makes decisions about local laws.

The state has the three branches of government. The three branches manage the government of the state. Our country has the three branches, too. These three branches take care of the laws of our country.

FACT BOX

There have been 43 different presidents of the United States up to 2008. The president leads the executive branch of government.

13

Checks and Balances

A government needs **checks and balances**. This means no branch of government has too much power. Each branch can do its job, but not the job of others.

Long ago, many countries were ruled by kings. A king had all the power in a country. He decided what people needed, but sometimes his choices were wrong. Checks and balances divide the power. One branch can keep another branch from making a bad decision.

This picture shows Bahadur Shah Zafar, the last emperor of India. Emperors and kings once ruled countries. They had all the power.

The Constitution gave Americans control of the government.

How do checks and balances work? Imagine your town wants to pass a new law. The law would say that no one can cut down a tree. The legislative branch can ask for the law. If the mayor thinks the law is a bad idea, he or she can say no to the law. If the mayor agrees to the law, a judge makes sure the law is fair and right.

Follow the Leaders

Every government has a leader. A city has a mayor. Each state has a governor. The president leads our country. They are the most well-known people in the government.

The mayor, governor, and president lead the executive branch of their government. They make sure things get done. They tell people to do what the law says. The leaders listen to advice from the legislative branch of government. They can also ask for new laws.

Abraham Lincoln was the 16th president of the United States.

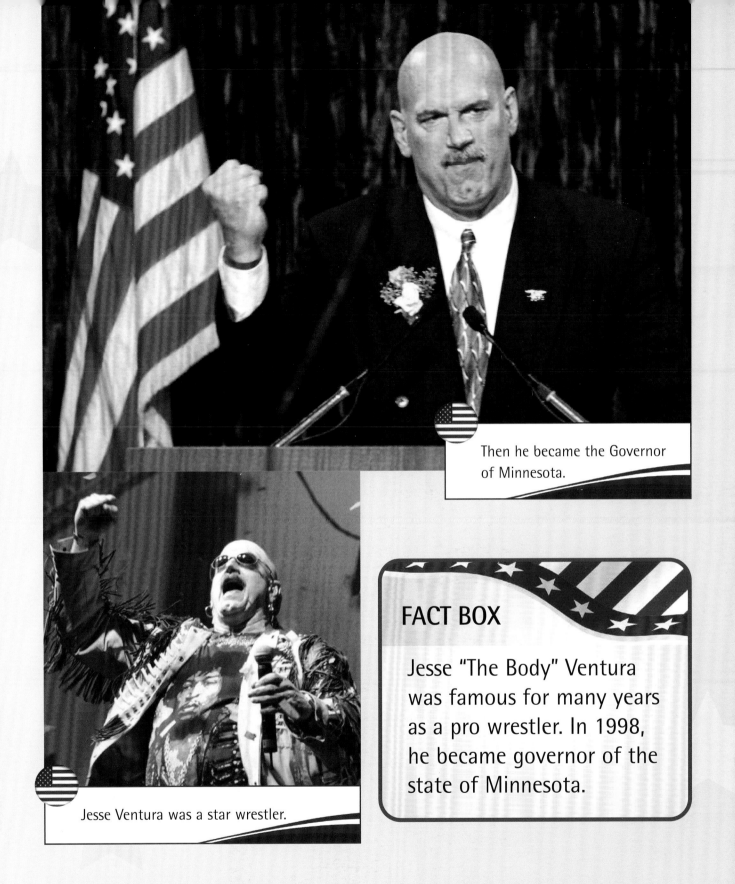

Then he became the Governor of Minnesota.

Jesse Ventura was a star wrestler.

FACT BOX

Jesse "The Body" Ventura was famous for many years as a pro wrestler. In 1998, he became governor of the state of Minnesota.

Mayors, governors, and the president become leaders by winning **elections**. In an elections, people vote for the leader they want. Each city and state decides how long someone can be a leader. The president leads the country for four years before the next election.

Making the Rules

Every government has a legislative branch. This branch makes new laws. If the leader of the executive branch agrees with their ideas, they become new laws.

Ideas for new laws can come from all people. People in the legislative branch talk about the ideas. They ask experts what they think. If enough people want to talk about a new law, the government may have special meetings with them. People can then explain why they like it or not.

A community government meets at the Town Hall to make new laws.

Our Congress has offices and meets here, at the Capitol.

Our national government is in Washington, D.C. The legislative branch there is called the United States Congress. Congress has 100 **senators**. There are two senators from each of the 50 states. The House of Representatives has over 400 members. There is at least one member from each state. Together, they form Congress. All of these men and women help make new laws for our country.

Law and Order

Our country has many courts, and each one has a judge. People who break the law go to court. The truth will be explained in court, and the judge decides what should happen. The court will also help if people do not agree about a law. The judge helps decide who is right or how the law should work. A judge decides what is fair.

You may have a court in your community. It serves the people in your town. Each state has its own courts. The government uses **federal** courts for problems important to the whole country. Each state has at least one federal court.

The scales are a symbol for our courts.

The nine members of the Supreme Court hear cases in this building.

The United States **Supreme Court** is the highest court in the country. It has nine judges. Only the most important cases go to the Supreme Court.

FACT BOX

People call the judges of the Supreme Court "Justices."

Health Care

If you do not feel well at school, you can see a school nurse. Your school also makes sure you get exercise. The government puts these programs in schools. They want you to be healthy.

People get sick or hurt. They see their doctor or go to a hospital. This can cost a lot of money. Some people do not have enough money to pay for medical care. The government has a plan called health care. This plan helps some children, the elderly, and the poor. The plan helps many people get the care they need.

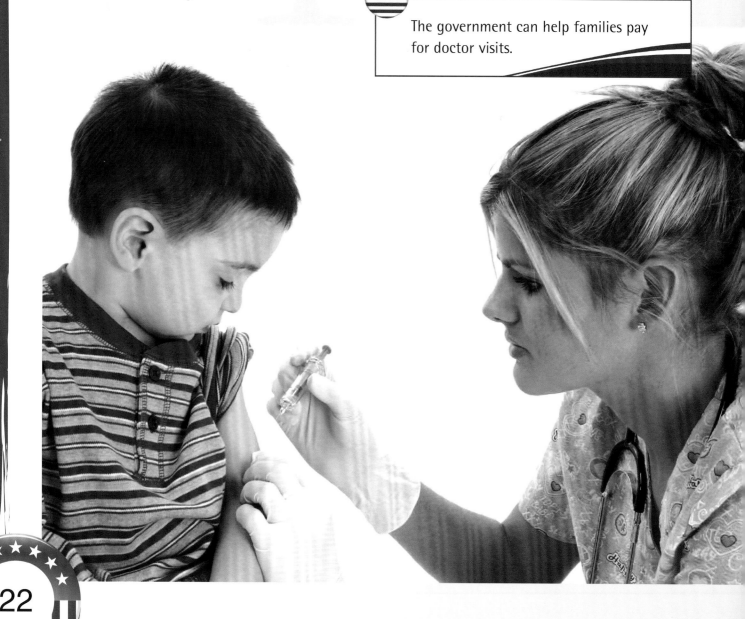

The government can help families pay for doctor visits.

Our government helps hospitals get expensive equipment.

The United States spends more money on health care than does any other country. Machines used for medical tests can cost a lot of money. The government helps with some of the cost. The government tests new medicines. It also helps doctors find cures for diseases.

The Post Office

The United States Postal Service is part of the executive branch of the government. It began in 1775, and is also called the post office. The post office handles all of our mail including the letters and bills we send. We pay for mail delivery by buying stamps. We place the stamps on letters and packages that we mail.

Post offices can be small or very large. A lot of mail goes to the large offices. People and machines sort all of it.

Post office workers deliver the mail. They walk to your mail box or bring it to you by truck.

The government charges a small amount to deliver letters.

Postal workers bring mail to homes and businesses six days a week.

Some pieces of mail are not small. For example, some people buy things that must be delivered through the mail. The post office can bring the larger packages right to their homes.

FACT BOX

You will find the smallest post office in the United States in Ochopee, Florida. The building used to be a shed on a tomato farm.

Our Environment

You see the environment all around us. It is the sky, the grass, the water, and the trees. We need these things to have a healthy life. We have also done much to harm the environment. We pollute the air and the water. We have cut down millions of trees. Garbage and litter cover many places.

The government knows this. Congress passes many laws to help our environment. They do not allow factories to pollute the air and water as much. The government also protects animals and the land.

The government makes companies like these limit the pollution they put in the air.

When people recycle, the government has less garbage to get rid of.

We can help the government in many ways. Do not litter. Try to recycle paper, glass, and plastic. Talk to your family and friends to get new ideas.

Read books about how to save the environment. If we work together with the government, we can all have a cleaner world.

The Treasury

We all use money. We have some with us almost all the time. It is not easy to live without it. Have you ever wondered where it comes from?

Our government started the United States Treasury. It makes all of our money. Two factories make the paper money. One is in Washington, D.C. and the other is in Fort Worth, Texas. Four different factories called a **mint** make all of the coins. You will find the largest mint in Philadelphia, Pennsylvania.

Our government prints all of the paper money we use.

The government watches how banks use money.

The Treasury manages all the money for the banks and the country. It also collects money paid to the government, called **taxes**. All taxes go to the Treasury. The government uses it like a giant bank.

FACT BOX

A $1 bill lasts about 18 months before the government replaces it with a new one. A $20 bill lasts about four years.

29

The Fun Side

You have probably played in a park. Some have nice playgrounds and gardens. Cities have libraries filled with books. We learn a lot by visiting a museum. You can have a lot of fun at the zoo, and you can stay cool at the beach. Many of these places would not be there without help from the government.

The government formed the National Park Service in 1916. It cares for all the **national parks** in our country. A national park is a natural part of our country that the government protects. For example, millions of people visit Yosemite National Park in California every year.

Community governments build parks for children to play in.

Cities and states run zoos for visitors to enjoy.

The government knows we work hard. It also knows we all want to have fun. We like going places with our friends and family. We want places to play and get exercise. We want to learn. We need these places if we want a better life. This makes our country strong.

Glossary

branches Different parts of a group

checks and balances When power is equal between different groups

community A group of people living in the same area

district A special government that has one specific job

election An event when people vote for their choice

executive The part of government that makes sure laws are obeyed

federal The government group in charge of the whole country

government The group in charge of a country, state, city, etc.

judge A person who is in charge of the court

judicial The part of government that make decisions in court

law A rule made by the government

legislative The part of government that makes laws

mayor The leader of a city government

military Army, navy, and air force people who protect the country

mint A factory that makes coins used for money

national parks Park land owned and protected by the government

senator A government leader who works in the legislative branch

Supreme Court The highest court in the United States

taxes The money people pay to the government

Index